From Your Friends at **The MAILBOX**®

Expressive

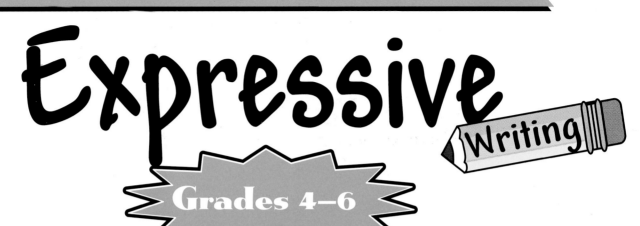

Writing

Grades 4–6

Project Manager:
Kim T. Griswell

Writers:
Lynn Tutterow and Lori Sammartino

Contributing Editors:
Cayce Guiliano, Deborah T. Kalwat,
Scott Lyons, Jennifer Munnerlyn

Art Coordinator:
Clevell Harris

Artists:
Pam Crane, Theresa Lewis Goode, Clevell Harris,
Susan Hodnett, Sheila Krill, Rob Mayworth,
Greg D. Rieves, Barry Slate, Donna K. Teal

Cover Artists:
Nick Greenwood and Kimberly Richard

www.themailbox.com

Writing Works!

©2000 by THE EDUCATION CENTER, INC.
All rights reserved.
ISBN #1-56234-371-8

Manufactured in the United States

10 9 8 7 6 5 4 3 2

Table of Contents

About This Book

What Is Expressive Writing?

In *expressive writing* a writer uses sensory detail and emotions to share experiences and insights regarding people, ideas, places, and things. The writer uses details that are specific and accurate. To provide specific and accurate details, the writer relies on all five senses: *sight, hearing, touch, taste,* and *smell. Sequence of events, point of view, detail, dialogue,* and *setting* are very important in expressive writing. Types of expressive writing include autobiographies, personal letters, diaries, journals, personal essays, travelogs, memoirs, learning logs, peer dialogues, and some forms of poetry.

Because expressive writing allows a student to write in his or her own words without fear of being "corrected," it is not meant to be graded (especially for grammar or mechanics). Instead, readers should offer supportive, nonjudgmental responses. Writing expressively on a regular basis has been shown to enhance self-esteem and build a positive attitude toward writing.

Develop and enhance your students' expressive-writing skills with this easy-to-use collection of 20 two-page lessons. *Writing Works!—Expressive* contains everything you need to supplement a successful writing program in your classroom.

Each two-page lesson contains the following:
- A motivating writing prompt
- Simple steps for teaching the prewriting and writing stages of each lesson
- A student reproducible that is either a graphic organizer used in the prewriting stages or a pattern on which students write their final drafts
- Suggestions for publishing or displaying students' work

Also included:
- A reproducible peer response sheet for the student
- A reproducible expressive-writing response sheet for the teacher
- 16 extra expressive-writing prompts
- A student reproducible containing 13 commonly used editing symbols

Other books in the Writing Works! series:
- *Writing Works!—Descriptive*
- *Writing Works!—Explanatory*
- *Writing Works!—Clarification*
- *Writing Works!—Persuasive*
- *Writing Works!—Narrative*

Painting With Words

PROMPT

Imagine that you are an artist who paints pictures with words instead of paint. Think of something that happened to you last year that made you sad, happy, fearful, or excited. Use descriptive words to help you paint a word picture of what happened.

Think It!

1. Tell students that just as an artist expresses his feelings by painting with different colors, a writer expresses his emotions by using colorful words. Read aloud each group of words below and ask students to identify the emotion described.

   dull, dark, blue *(sadness)*   cold, heavy, dark *(fear)*

   rosy, warm, sunny *(happiness)*   wild, waving, breathless *(excitement)*

2. Share with students a time when you were sad, happy, excited, or fearful. Tell students what your experience smelled, tasted, sounded, felt, and looked like.

3. Explain to students that expressive writing uses sensory details and emotions to share experiences and insights regarding people, ideas, places, and things. Then read aloud the prompt above, display it on a transparency, or write it on the board.

4. Give each student a copy of page 5. Direct the student to use the reproducible to list descriptive words that express his feelings about a time when he was sad, happy, fearful, or excited.

Write It!

1. Instruct each student to use the sensory details he listed on page 5 to help him write a memoir. Inform students that a memoir is an event or story told from personal experience. Further explain that the event or story should include specific and accurate details about what happened, when it happened, where it happened, and to whom it happened.

2. Encourage students to swap papers for peer response. After all changes have been made, direct the student to write the final version of his memoir on a construction paper cutout of a painter's palette.

3. Finally, have each student dip his thumb in various paint colors and make thumbprints around his palette. Display the finished products on a bulletin board titled "Painting With Words."

Painting With Words

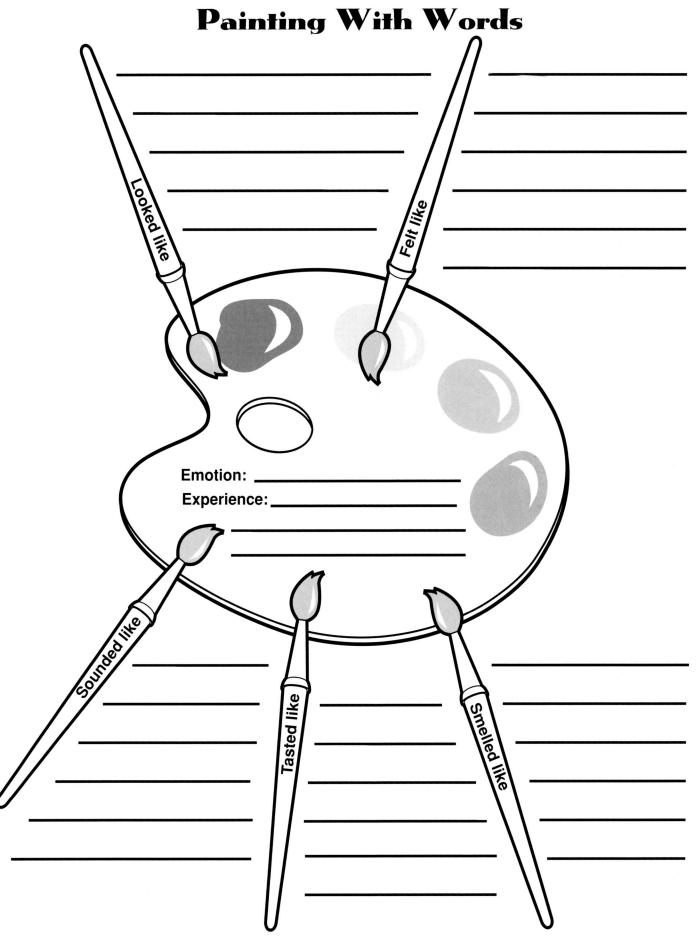

Looked like

Felt like

Emotion: _____

Experience: _____

_____

_____

Sounded like

Tasted like

Smelled like

Poetry Quilts

PROMPT

If you could use only ten words to write your life story, which words would you choose? Write your own autobiography in the form of a poem.

Think It!

1. Share with students highlights from your life that you would include in an autobiographical poem. Ask student volunteers to share some of their highlights.

2. Explain to your students that expressive writing uses sensory detail and emotions to share experiences and insights regarding people, ideas, places, and things. Then read aloud the prompt above, display it on a transparency, or write it on the board.

3. Instruct each student to make a list on a sheet of paper of personal traits, such as nouns that tell about her, adjectives that describe her, and verbs that tell about things she likes to do.

Write It!

1. Direct the student to use her list to write an autobiographical poem using the following guidelines. The first line should be an article and one noun that tells about her. The second line should be one adjective, one conjunction (joining word), and one adjective describing her. The third line should be one verb, one conjunction, and one verb telling about the things she likes to do. The fourth line should be one adverb referring back to the third line. The last line should be the student's name. Remind the student that in expressive writing, the writer relies on all five senses: sight, sound, touch, taste, and smell.

2. Encourage students to swap papers for peer response. After all changes have been made, give each student a piece of 9" x 12" construction paper, as well as a copy of page 7 on which to write her finished poem.

3. After each student writes her poem on page 7, instruct her to color the quilt border. Then have her cut along the bold cutting line and glue her quilt square onto the construction paper. Staple students' final products together along the edges to create a quilt and display it on a wall with the title "Poetry Quilt" in the middle.

Name _____

Poetry Quilts

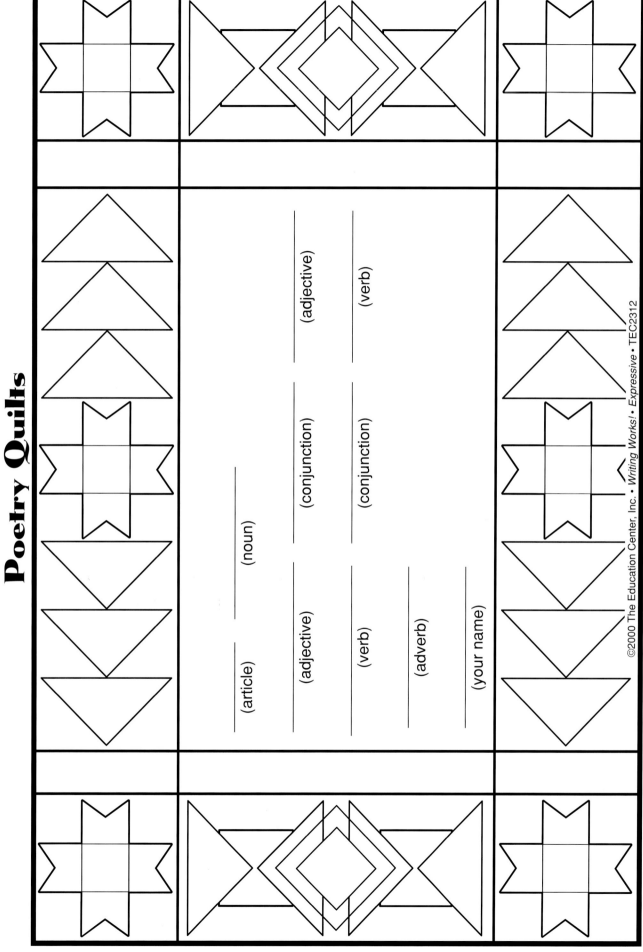

_____ _____
(article) (noun)

_____ _____
(adjective) (conjunction)

_____ _____
(verb) (adjective)

_____ _____
(adverb) (conjunction)

_____ _____
(your name) (verb)

©2000 The Education Center, Inc. • *Writing Works!* • *Expressive* • TEC2312

7

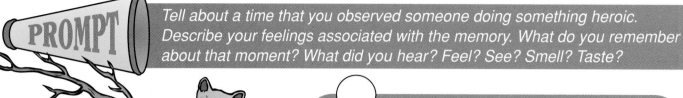

Now That's a Hero!

PROMPT *Tell about a time that you observed someone doing something heroic. Describe your feelings associated with the memory. What do you remember about that moment? What did you hear? Feel? See? Smell? Taste?*

Think It!

1. Discuss with your students what a hero is. Ask your class to compare a comic book superhero with a real-life hero. What are their similarities? Differences? With your students, brainstorm acts of heroism and record them on the board.

2. Explain to your students that *expressive writing* uses sensory detail and emotions to share experiences and insights regarding people, ideas, places, and things. Then read aloud the prompt above, display it on a transparency, or write it on the board.

3. Give each student a copy of page 9. Direct him to use the reproducible to help gather his thoughts about the hero and his heroic deed. Have the student load up the hero sandwich with details about the hero's deed and the student's feelings about that deed.

Write It!

1. Have each student use the information recorded on page 9 to help him write a personal letter to his hero on another sheet of paper. Inform students that a personal letter has five parts: a *heading,* a *salutation* or greeting, a *body,* a *closing,* and a *signature.* Have the student write the address and the date in the top right-hand corner of the letter (heading) and greet his hero (salutation). Then have him write about the heroic deed that he observed and how it made him feel, including as many details and memories associated with the incident as he can recall (body). Have the student include a closing word or phrase, such as "Sincerely" or "Love," keeping in mind to whom he is writing the letter (closing). Then have the student sign the letter underneath the closing (signature).

2. Encourage students to swap papers for peer response. After all changes have been made, direct each student to write the final version of his personal letter on a sheet of stationery.

3. Bring in lemonade or another special beverage to celebrate these special heroes. Then have each student serve up (read!) his letter as a special literary treat for the entire class. Encourage each student, if possible, to mail or give the letter to the person about whom he wrote. Now *that's* a hero!

Now That's a Hero!

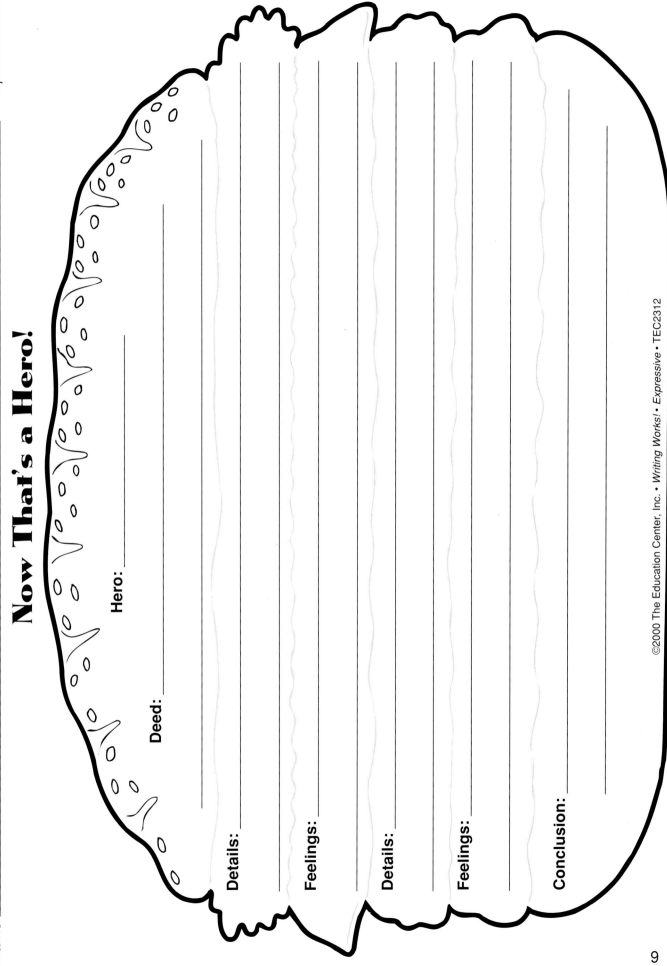

Hero: _____

Deed: _____

Details: _____

Feelings: _____

Details: _____

Feelings: _____

Conclusion: _____

Amusement Park Lark

PROMPT

Recall a time when you visited an amusement park, carnival, or fair. Think of all the fun you had during your visit! Write a journal entry about your experience.

Think It!

1. Have students close their eyes while you tell about a trip to an amusement park. Use sensory details to describe your experience, including things you saw, heard, smelled, tasted, and felt.

2. Explain to your students that expressive writing uses sensory details and emotions to share experiences and insights regarding people, ideas, places, and things. Then read aloud the prompt above, display it on a transparency, or write it on the board.

3. Give each student a copy of page 11 and instruct her to use the reproducible to list strong, active words that are related to the sights, sounds, smells, tastes, and feelings of an amusement park.

Write It!

1. Instruct each student to use the information on page 11 to help her write a journal entry using the sensory details she listed. Explain that the journal entry should include specific and accurate details about her personal thoughts, feelings, and experiences.

2. Encourage students to swap papers for peer response. After all changes have been made, direct the student to write the final version of her journal entry on another sheet of paper.

3. Display the students' writing on a bulletin board titled "Amusement Park Lark."

Name _____

Amusement Park Lark

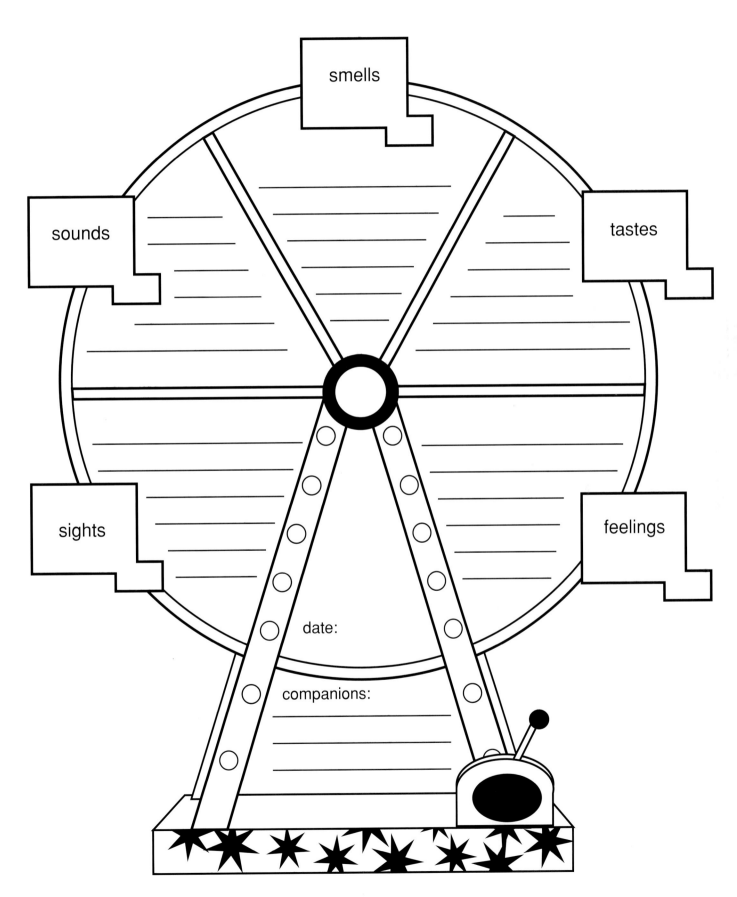

smells

sounds

tastes

sights

feelings

date:

companions:

What I Think

PROMPT *Pretend your school newspaper has asked you to be a reporter. Your first assignment is to write an editorial describing your opinion about a school issue or event.*

Think It!

1. Have each student brainstorm and record at least three school issues or events that he would like to inform his classmates about.

2. Describe an issue or event of your own to students. Then challenge them to recount the issue or event by telling who was involved, what happened, when it happened, where it happened, and why it happened.

3. Explain to students that expressive writing uses sensory details and emotions to share experiences and insights regarding people, ideas, places, and things. Then read aloud the prompt above, display it on a transparency, or write it on the board.

4. Give each student a copy of page 13. Direct the student to choose one of the issues or events he generated earlier to detail on the reproducible.

Write It!

1. Instruct each student to use the information he listed on page 13 to help him write an editorial. Inform students that in an editorial the writer tells his opinion about an issue or event. Further explain that an editorial should include specific and accurate details about what the writer thinks and feels about what happened, when it happened, where it happened, who was involved, and why it happened.

2. Encourage students to swap papers for peer response. After all changes have been made, direct the student to write the final version of his editorial on a sheet of lined paper or on a large index card.

3. Finally, have each student read his editorial to the class as if he were a reporter.

Name____

What I Think

School Voice

Volume 1 Issue 1

What happened:

____
____
____
____
____
____

When it happened:

____
____
____
____
____
____

Where it happened:

____
____

Who was involved:

____
____
____
____
____
____

Why it happened:

____
____
____
____
____
____

Free-Flying Poetry

PROMPT *Poets carefully select words that evoke feelings and mental pictures in the reader or listener. Use word pictures and pleasing sounds to write a free-verse poem about one of the following topics:* friendship, courage, happiness, *or* beauty.

Think It!

1. With your students, brainstorm word associations with the first day of summer vacation or the first snow of the year. Record their responses on the board. Tell students that word pictures such as these are especially helpful in conveying a mood or feeling.

2. Explain to your students that expressive writing uses sensory detail and emotions to share experiences and insights regarding people, ideas, places, and things. Then read aloud the prompt above, display it on a transparency, or write it on the board.

3. Give each student a copy of page 15. Then provide the students with the following directions:
   — Write your topic in the space provided.
   — Write words or phrases that paint pictures of that topic on the provided lines on the kite.
   — After a few minutes, look for a central thread in your thoughts. Write that central thought down as the summary.
   — From the summary, brainstorm another group of words in the provided spaces on the kite tail.

   If a student's brainstorming becomes blocked, prompt her to describe the topic by listing what it looks, sounds, smells, and feels like, or have her compare it to a person, place, or thing.

Write It!

1. Have each student use the information recorded on page 15 to write, on another sheet of paper, a free-verse poem about her chosen topic. Inform students that *free verse* is poetry without rules about rhyme or meter. Share examples of free verse with your students (Carl Sandburg's "Fog" is a good choice). Instruct each student to select from the reproducible the words and phrases she wishes to use for her poem. Then have her write a short paragraph using those word pictures. To create her poem, she adds line breaks to her paragraph. At first, have her make the breaks where they seem to naturally fall, and then continue moving words or phrases until the poem sounds right to her. Instruct her to add, delete, or change words as necessary.

2. Encourage students to swap papers for peer response. After all changes have been made, direct each student to write the final version of her free verse on another sheet of paper.

3. Cut a class supply of colorful 12" x 18" sheets of construction paper into 12" squares. After distributing the squares, have each student turn hers diagonally so that it looks like a kite, cut out her poem, and paste it onto the square. Direct students to make kite tails with yarn and glue them onto their kites. After the glue dries, hang the poems from the ceiling and title the display "Free-Flying Poetry."

Free-Flying Poetry

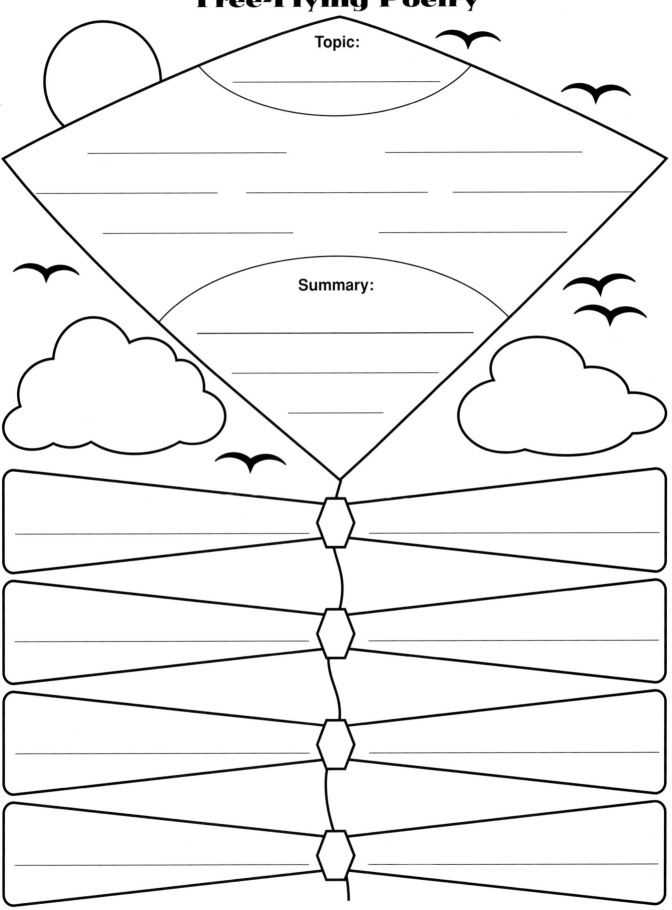

Topic:

_____

_____   _____
_____
_____   _____

Summary:

_____

_____

_____

My Life's Highway

PROMPT — *Take a trip down the highway of your life. Think about the people you have met and experiences that you have had along the way. Write a memoir about one of your most vivid memories or dreams for the future.*

Think It!

1. Have students brainstorm life experiences. Encourage them to share details about family members, friends, favorite things, important school events, special abilities, hobbies and interests, and future dreams.

2. Explain to your students that expressive writing uses sensory details and emotions to share experiences and insights regarding people, ideas, places, and things. Then read aloud the prompt above, display it on a transparency, or write it on the board.

3. Give each student a copy of page 17 and have him use the reproducible to write notes about his life experiences and his dreams for the future. Encourage him to use sensory details and emotions related to his experiences.

Write It!

1. Explain that a memoir is a written record of the writer's own experience. Instruct each student to use the details (recorded on page 17) to help him write a memoir. Encourage him to use specific and accurate details about his life experiences and dreams for the future.

2. Have students swap papers for peer response. After all changes have been made, direct the student to write the final version of his memoir on a 5" x 8" sheet of paper.

3. Have students make license plates by cutting 6" x 9" tagboard rectangles. Allow time for them to illustrate their license plates with decorative borders. Glue the memoirs to the center of the plates. Enlarge the road signs and pictures shown on page 17 and have students color them. Create a bulletin board titled "Driving Life's Highway" with a drawing of a road, the road signs, and pictures. Display the license plate memoirs for everyone to enjoy.

My Life's Highway

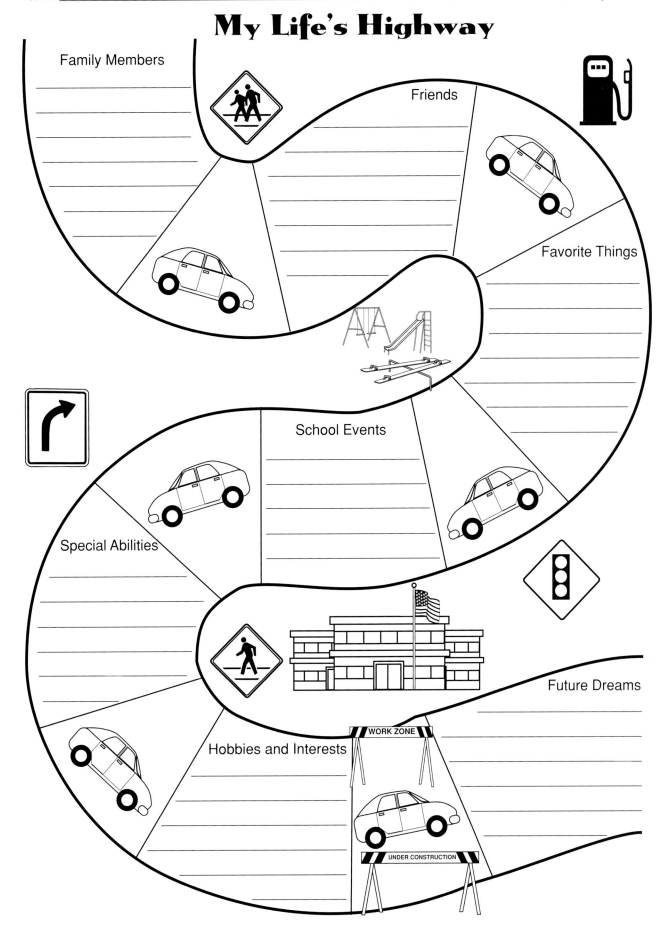

Family Members

Friends

Favorite Things

School Events

Special Abilities

Future Dreams

Hobbies and Interests

WORK ZONE

UNDER CONSTRUCTION

And the Award Goes to...

Imagine a movie was made about this past year of your life. Who has played a supporting role in making your year a success? Write a thank-you speech about this person.

Think It!

1. Share with students a person who has taken on a supporting role in this past year for you, such as a family member, co-worker, friend, or administrator. Explain what this person has done for you or has meant to you.

2. Ask student volunteers to share personal accounts about people who have been supportive to them.

3. Explain to students that expressive writing uses sensory details and emotions to share experiences and insights regarding people, ideas, places, and things. Then read aloud the prompt above, display it on a transparency, or write it on the board.

4. Give each student a copy of page 19. Direct the student to use the reproducible to help plan her speech about the person who has played a supporting role in her life this past year.

Write It!

1. Instruct the student to use the information recorded on page 19 to help her write a thank-you speech about her supporting person. Explain to students that in expressive writing the writer uses details that are specific and accurate, such as sequence of events, point of view, and setting.

2. Encourage students to swap papers for peer response. After all changes have been made, direct the student to write the final version of her speech on another sheet of paper.

3. Give each student a piece of 9" x 12" construction paper. Instruct her to design an award giving the details of why her person has earned such an award. Then, if possible, invite the student's supporting person to the class and have the student give her speech as she presents the award. Display final versions and awards on a bulletin board titled "And the Award Goes to…"

And the Award Goes to...

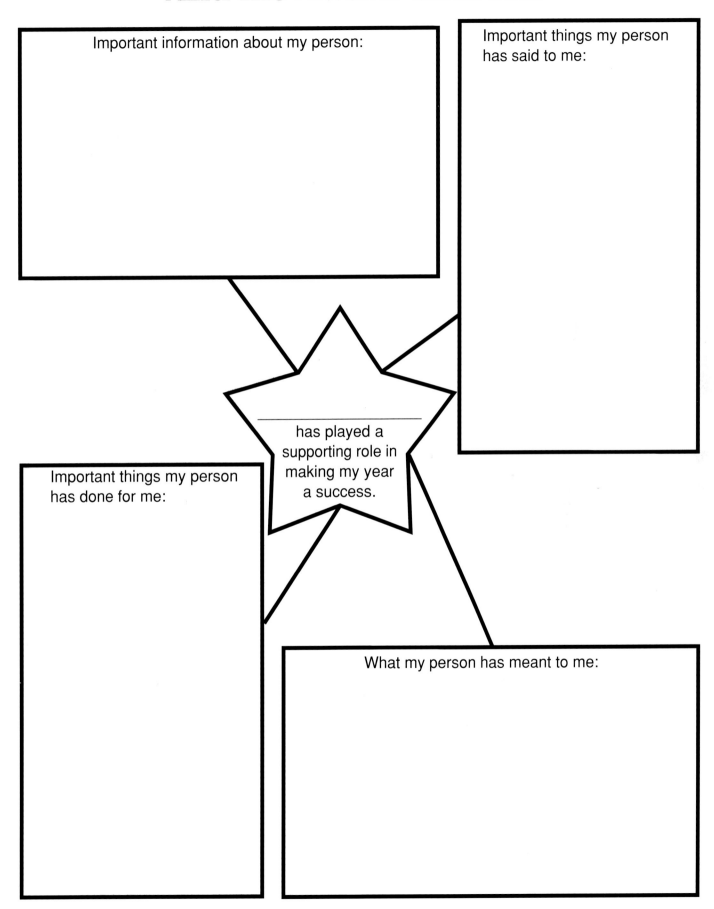

Important information about my person:

Important things my person has said to me:

_____

has played a supporting role in making my year a success.

Important things my person has done for me:

What my person has meant to me:

Sailing the High Seas

PROMPT *Imagine that you are going on an imaginary cruise. Write a travelog giving the details of your adventure.*

Think It!

1. Have students close their eyes and imagine sailing on a ship. Direct them to think about what they see, touch, hear, smell, taste, and feel inside. Ask student volunteers to share what they are experiencing on their imaginary journeys.

2. Explain to students that expressive writing uses sensory details and emotions to share experiences and insights regarding people, ideas, places, and things. Then read aloud the prompt above, display it on a transparency, or write it on the board.

3. Give each student a copy of page 21. Direct the student to use the reproducible to list all of the sensory and emotional experiences he thinks he would feel if he were actually on the cruise.

Write It!

1. Instruct each student to use the information recorded on page 21 to help write his travelog. Remind the student to use sensory details and feelings that are specific and accurate.

2. Encourage students to swap papers for peer response. After all changes have been made, direct the student to write the final version of his travelog on another sheet of paper.

3. Give each student a piece of brown construction paper. Direct him to cut the paper to look like an old travelog found on a ship (see page 21 for an example). Then have him glue his final version to the construction paper. Display students' travelogs on a bulletin board titled "Sailing the High Seas."

Name ______________________

Sailing the High Seas

I see ______________________

____

____

____

I hear ______________________

____

____

____

I smell ______________________

____

____

____

I touch ______________________

____

____

____

I taste ______________________

____

____

____

Inside, I feel ______________________

____

____

____

The Perfect Place

PROMPT

Imagine you are going on a trip to either your favorite place or somewhere you have always wanted to go. Write a cinquain poem about this place.

Think It!

1. Have each student brainstorm a list of her favorite places or places she would like to visit, such as states, countries, or landmarks. Provide students with magazines, travel brochures, or other resource materials to browse through for ideas.

2. Introduce students to the cinquain form of poetry. On a chalkboard or chart paper list the following information about a cinquain:
   - It is a five-line poem based on syllables.
   - Line 1—one word with two syllables (place)
   - Line 2—four syllables (describing the place)
   - Line 3—six syllables (showing action at the place)
   - Line 4—eight syllables (expressing feelings or observations about the place)
   - Line 5—two syllables (describing or renaming the place)

3. Explain to students that expressive writing uses sensory details and emotions to share experiences and insights regarding people, ideas, places, and things. Then read aloud the prompt above, display it on a transparency, or write it on the board.

4. Give each student a copy of page 23. Direct the student to choose one of the places she listed earlier to write about on the top half of the reproducible.

Write It!

1. Instruct each student to use the information she listed on the top of page 23 to help her write a cinquain on another sheet of paper. Remind students that their cinquains should follow the syllable guidelines listed.

2. Encourage students to swap papers for peer response. After all changes have been made, direct the student to write the final version of her cinquain on the bottom of page 23.

3. Finally, have each student cut out her cinquain and glue it in the center of an 18" x 12" sheet of light-colored construction paper. Instruct each student to use various art supplies to transform her sheet into a travel poster.

The Perfect Place

Place: _____

Describe the place: _____

_____

_____

Actions/events: _____

_____

_____

Feelings/observations: _____

_____

Other names for the place: _____

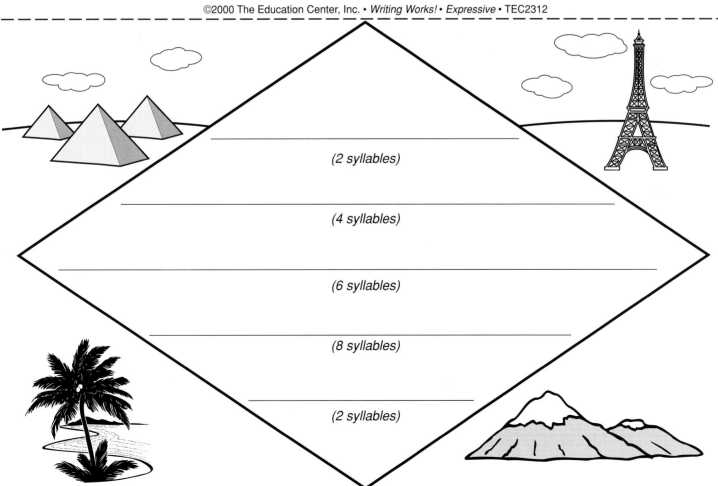

_____

(2 syllables)

_____

(4 syllables)

_____

(6 syllables)

_____

(8 syllables)

_____

(2 syllables)

What's the Buzz?

PROMPT

What is your teacher up to as she buzzes about the room helping students, teaching, taking notes, and talking with other teachers? Observe your teacher for the day and, in a learning log, record her actions and your thoughts about what she is doing.

Think It!

1. Walk around the room moving things from place to place and talking to students. Then ask students to recount your actions. Write student responses on the board. Then ask students to explain why they think you were doing each thing. Explain that for a student to create a learning log, he must observe someone else and make inferences about that person's actions.

2. Explain to students that expressive writing uses sensory details and emotions to share experiences and insights regarding people, ideas, places, and things. Then read aloud the prompt above, display it on a transparency, or write it on the board.

3. Give each student a copy of page 25. Direct the student to use the left-hand column of the learning log to record your actions for the day.

Write It!

1. After all observations have been recorded, instruct the student to use the right-hand column of the learning log on page 25 to write the reasons he thinks you have for doing each of the items listed in the left-hand column.

2. Collect students' learning logs and staple them together to create a class learning log. Create and attach a front and back cover. Title your class book "What's the Buzz About [teacher's name]?"

What's the Buzz?

My Thoughts

What is my teacher up to?
Action

Time

©2000 The Education Center, Inc. • *Writing Works!* • *Expressive* • TEC2312

Take a Walk in My Shoes

PROMPT *Imagine that your shoes could talk. Think about a special event in your life. Write a limerick telling about this event from your shoes' point of view.*

Think It!

1. Brainstorm types of shoes with students. List student responses on the board. Then ask students in what events each type of shoe would be worn. Write student responses on the board next to the appropriate shoe.

2. Explain to students that expressive writing uses sensory details and emotions to share experiences and insights regarding people, ideas, places, and things. Then read aloud the prompt above, display it on a transparency, or write it on the board.

3. Give each student a copy of page 27. Instruct the student to use the reproducible to help organize her thoughts about the special event from her shoes' point of view.

Write It!

1. Direct each student to use the information recorded on page 27 to help write a limerick about a special event from her shoes' point of view. Explain that a limerick is a poem with five lines. Lines one, two, and five have three stressed syllables each and rhyme; lines two and three have two stressed syllables each and rhyme. Also explain that expressive writing uses specific and accurate details that rely on the five senses.

2. Encourage students to swap papers for peer response. After all changes have been made, instruct the student to write the final version of her limerick on a sheet of paper.

3. Allow each student to share her limerick. Then have her draw a picture of the event from her shoes' point of view. Remind the student to think about where her shoes are and how they would look up at everything. Display limericks and pictures on a bulletin board titled "Take a Walk in My Shoes."

Take a Walk in My Shoes

What I think about this event:

What I touch:

Special event:

What I see:

What I smell:

What I hear:

Type of shoe I am:

Larger Than Life

PROMPT

Have you ever wondered what would happen if a common everyday object suddenly started to grow and grow and grow? Write a journal entry about a time when something you owned began to grow.

Think It!

1. Instruct each student to select an object from his desk, such as a pencil, penny, eraser, ruler, or crayon.

2. Direct each student to close his eyes and imagine that the common everyday object he has chosen is starting to grow. Ask him if it still feels the same, if it has a smell, if he can hear it growing, and if the object can still be used. Tell him to imagine that the object is the size of a house and that he is walking around inside it. Tell him to continue to observe the differences in his object as he walks around in it. Then tell him to walk through the other side and open his eyes.

3. Explain to students that expressive writing uses sensory details and emotions to share experiences and insights regarding people, ideas, places, and things. Then read aloud the prompt above, display it on a transparency, or write it on the board.

4. Instruct students to choose an object to write about. Then give each student a copy of page 29. Direct him to use the reproducible to brainstorm sensory images about the object that kept growing.

Write It!

1. Have each student use the information on page 29 to help write his journal entry. Remind him to use specific and accurate details using the five senses. Further remind him that sequence of events, point of view, details and setting are very important in expressive writing.

2. Encourage students to swap papers for peer response. After all changes have been made, direct the student to write the final version of his journal entry on another sheet of paper.

3. Give each student a 12" x 18" sheet of construction paper. Instruct him to draw a picture of his object as large as possible and then cut it out. Next have him tape his final version to the bottom edge of the object. Punch one or more holes in the top of the object; then tie a length of string through the holes. Hang students' final products from the ceiling.

Larger Than Life

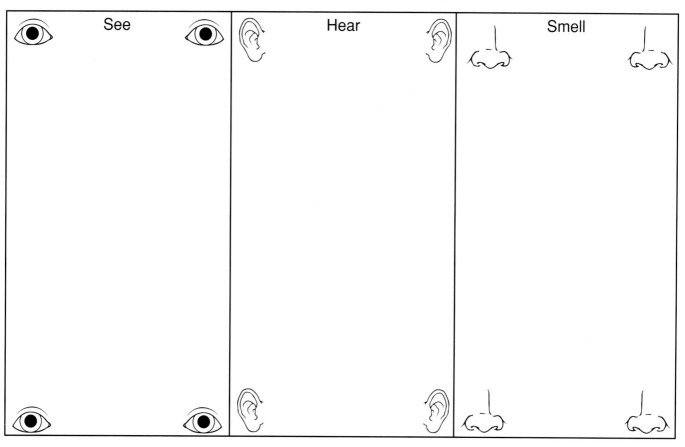

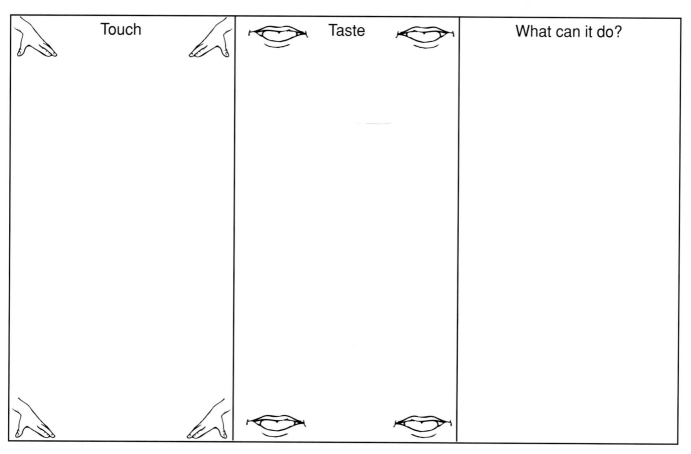

I'm a Little Teapot?

PROMPT *If you were an object, what object would you be? In a personal essay, tell what it's like to be the object you've chosen by explaining where you go, what you see and do, how you feel, and what others think of you.*

Think It!

1. With your students, brainstorm a list of everyday objects (a telephone, a toaster, a car, a book, etc.). Record their responses on the board. Have students think about how these objects work or how they're used. For instance, microwaves cook things quickly, though sometimes unevenly.

2. Have students think about how their personalities might be similar to how an object functions. Give them an example like the following: I'm like a microwave because I do my work quickly, and microwaves cook and heat things quickly.

3. Explain to your students that expressive writing uses sensory detail and emotions to share experiences and insights regarding people, ideas, places, and things. Then read aloud the prompt above, display it on a transparency, or write it on the board.

4. Give each student a copy of page 31. Have students carefully choose the object they are most like. Then have them use the reproducible to organize their thoughts and feelings.

Write It!

1. Instruct each student to use the information recorded on page 31 to write, on another sheet of paper, a personal essay about a day in the life of the object she's chosen. Have her include the feelings, thoughts, and sensations that she, as that object, experiences.

2. Encourage students to swap papers for peer response. After all changes have been made, direct each student to write the final version of her personal essay on another sheet of paper.

3. Have each student draw a large outline of her object on a 12" x 18" piece of light-colored construction paper. Then direct each student to glue the final version of her personal essay inside that outline, trimming as needed. (If a student doesn't have enough space to glue her essay inside the outline, tell her to rewrite it inside the outline instead.) Have her cut out construction paper arms, legs, ears, and hair and glue them to her object. Place the students' finished products on a bulletin board titled "I'm a Little Teapot?"

I'm a Little Teapot?

What I See:

What Others Think of Me:

Where I Go:

What I Do:

The object I am most like is a(n) _____

How I Feel:

Looking Back From the Future

PROMPT *What do you hope your life will be like in 20 years? Imagine yourself as a grown-up at a class reunion. Write a dialogue telling your classmates as many details about your grown-up life as possible.*

Welcome to Your 20th Class Reunion!

Think It!

1. With your students, brainstorm a list of people they admire. Record their responses on the board. The list may include sports or television celebrities, authors, or local citizens. Beside each name write some outstanding quality the person possesses.

2. Explain to your students that expressive writing uses sensory details and emotions to share experiences and insights regarding people, ideas, places, and things. Then read aloud the prompt above, display it on a transparency, or write it on the board.

3. Have students imagine themselves as grown-ups. Encourage them to imagine that they have some of the outstanding qualities they admire in others.

4. Give each student a copy of page 33. Direct the student to use the reproducible to organize his thoughts about the conversation in which he responds to questions about his experiences as an adult. Encourage him to use sensory details and emotions to express his goals and dreams for the future.

Write It!

1. Instruct the student to use the information on page 33 to help him write his dialogue on another sheet of paper. Remind the student that in expressive writing sequence of events, point of view, detail, and setting are very important.

2. Encourage students to swap papers for peer response. After all changes have been made, have the student write his final copy on another sheet of paper.

3. Have each student choose a partner to help him present his dialogue. Allow a few minutes for each pair to practice before performing the conversations for the class.

4. If desired, provide each student with an envelope in which to store his dialogue. Tell him to put the envelope in a safe place. When he is older he can open it and compare his childhood dreams with his adult accomplishments.

Expressive writing

Looking Back From the Future

Welcome to Your
20th Class Reunion!

"Hi there! I haven't seen you since we were kids!"

"What are you doing these days?"

"Who are the important people in your life now?"

"When did you get your first job and what was it?"

"Where do you live?"

"How have your experiences changed your life?"

"Why do you think you have been so successful?"

"What are you hoping to achieve in the future?"

Don't Try It in Your Diet!

PROMPT *Think of a time when you ate a really revolting food or imagine eating a disgusting dish. Write a rhyming poem about your real or imagined experience using words that tell how the food looked, smelled, and tasted.*

Appetizing Pizza
Yogurt-covered grasshoppers,
Chocolate-covered ants,
Crunchy, candied ladybugs
With sliced and diced eggplants,
These were on my pizza pie.
Mom said they'd be delicious.
But I suspect that was a lie.
They're probably just nutritious!

Think It!

1. Tell students that poets express their feelings and experiences with carefully chosen words that produce vivid images or mental pictures for those who read or listen to the poems.

2. Share a personal experience about a food that you found distasteful. Elaborate with details about the food's taste, appearance, texture, and odor. Ask students to recall the sensory details you shared. Write these on the board. Then model the process of using the details to write a short rhyming poem about your experience.

3. Explain to your students that expressive writing uses sensory details and emotions to share experiences and insights regarding people, ideas, places, and things. Then read aloud the prompt above, display it on a transparency, or write it on the board.

4. Give each student a copy of page 35 and instruct her to use the reproducible to list strong words that are related to the sights, sounds, smells, tastes, and feelings she experienced while eating a repulsive food. Remind writers that using a thesaurus or rhyming dictionary may be helpful in developing their poems.

Write It!

1. Instruct each student to use the information on page 35 to help her write a rhyming poem about the disgusting food on another sheet of paper. Have students include specific and accurate details about how the food looked, smelled, tasted, and felt to them while they were eating it.

2. Encourage students to swap papers for peer response. After all changes have been made, direct the student to write the final version of her poem on another sheet of paper.

3. Finally, give each student a paper plate. Have her illustrate her food using crayons or markers. Display the poems and illustrations along the cafeteria wall under the title "Don't Try It in Your Diet."

Don't Try It in Your Diet!

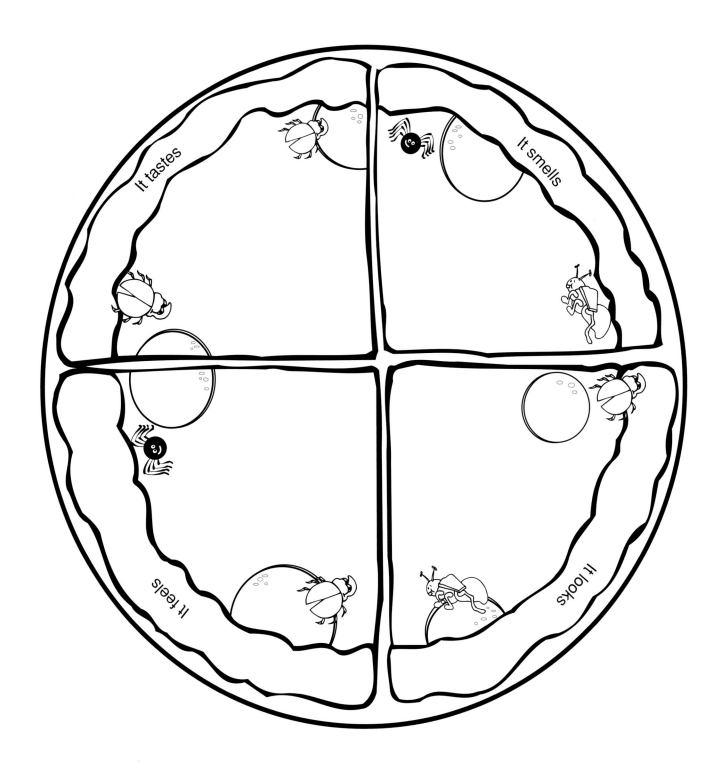

It tastes

It smells

It feels

It looks

Talk About a Great Road Trip!

PROMPT *Imagine that you and a friend are going on a cross-country car trip. Write a conversation between yourself and your friend planning the details of your trip.*

Think It!

1. Ask student volunteers to share with the class any trips they have taken. List city and state names on the board.

2. Discuss with students items they would need if traveling long distances by car, such as a map, food, money, and gas. Then discuss the types of plans they would need to make, such as how often to stop for food and gas and how long the trip will take.

3. Explain to your students that expressive writing uses sensory detail and emotions to share experiences and insights regarding people, ideas, places, and things. Then read aloud the prompt above, display it on a transparency, or write it on the board.

4. Give each student a copy of page 37. Direct the student to use the reproducible to organize his thoughts about the conversation between himself and his friend as they plan their cross-country trip.

Write It!

1. Instruct the student to use the information on page 37 to help write his conversation. Remind the student that sequence of events, point of view, detail, dialogue, and setting are very important in expressive writing.

2. Encourage students to swap papers for peer response. After all changes have been made, give each student a piece of white construction paper. Direct him to cut the paper into the shape of a speech bubble and write the final version of his conversation on one side of the bubble.

3. Prior to this activity, ask several student volunteers to bring suitcases to class. Display students' speech bubbles by taping them to the suitcases. Title the display "Talk About a Great Road Trip!"

Talk About a Great Road Trip!

Cities and states we'll drive through:

Things we'll see:

Items we'll need to take with us:

When we'll leave:
_____

How long we'll be gone:

When we'll be back:
_____

Places we'll visit:

37

Rainy Days

PROMPT *Imagine that you are standing under a shelter during a rainstorm. Write a journal entry about the rain using your five senses.*

Think It!

1. Share with students a time when you watched the snow falling or the sun shining. Describe how you felt using the five senses: sight, hearing, touch, taste, and smell.

2. Ask student volunteers to share similar experiences with the class. Remind them to use the five senses in their descriptions.

3. Explain to students that expressive writing uses sensory details and emotions to share experiences and insights regarding people, ideas, places, and things. Then read aloud the prompt above, display it on a transparency, or write it on the board.

4. Give each student a copy of page 39. Direct the student to use the reproducible to list descriptive words that express her feelings about the rainstorm.

Write It!

1. Instruct each student to use the sensory details she listed on page 39 to help her write her journal entry. Explain that expressive writing provides specific and accurate details using the five senses.

2. Encourage students to swap papers for peer response. After all changes have been made, direct the student to write the final version of her journal entry on a sheet of paper.

3. Give each student a 9" x 12" sheet of white construction paper. Have the student cut out a raindrop shape slightly smaller than the sheet and glue her final version to one side. Then have her punch a hole in the top of it, attach a length of string, and hang it from the ceiling for a rain shower right in the classroom.

Rainy Days

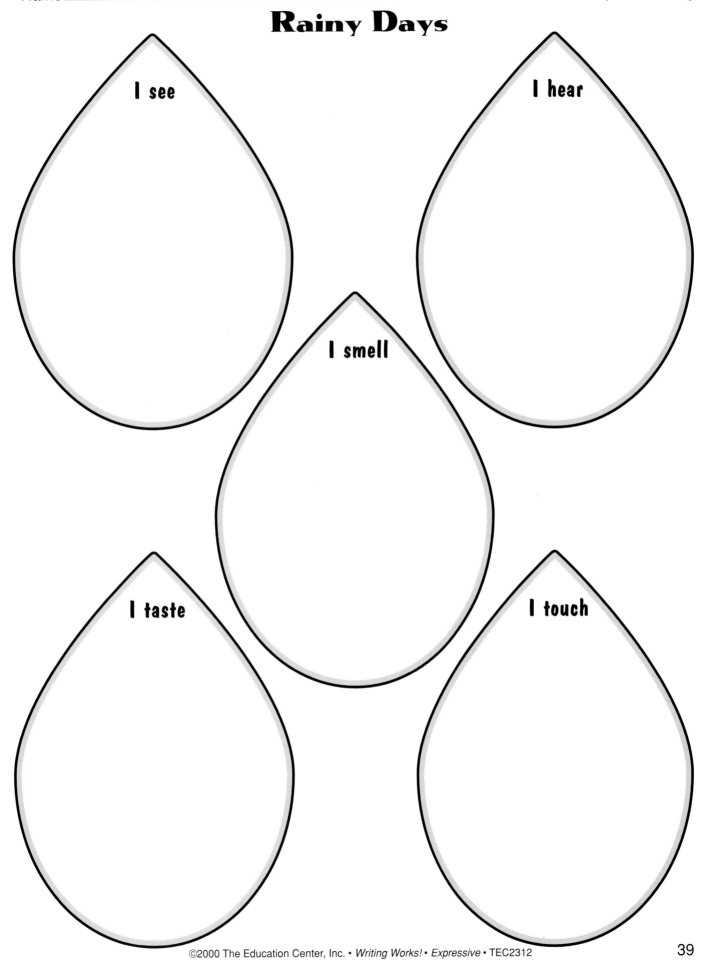

I see

I hear

I smell

I taste

I touch

Turning Points

PROMPT When people have experiences that change their lives, they call those experiences turning points. Write a journal entry about an event that has been a turning point in your life and explain how you changed.

Think It!

1. Discuss with students a personal turning point in your life. It might be a marriage, the birth of a child, a move, etc. Don't forget to describe how you felt. Then have students share some of their own turning points. Events such as hitting a home run, changing schools, or making a new friend can be milestones in a young person's life. Record their responses on the board.

2. Explain to your students that expressive writing uses sensory detail and emotions to share experiences and insights regarding people, ideas, places, and things. Then read aloud the prompt above, display it on a transparency, or write it on the board.

3. Give each student a copy of page 41. Direct him to use the reproducible to help gather and organize his thoughts.

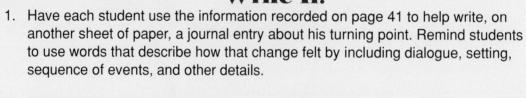

Write It!

1. Have each student use the information recorded on page 41 to help write, on another sheet of paper, a journal entry about his turning point. Remind students to use words that describe how that change felt by including dialogue, setting, sequence of events, and other details.

2. Encourage students to swap papers for peer response. After all changes have been made, direct each student to write the final version of his journal entry on another sheet of paper.

3. For proper display, have each student follow these directions: (a) turn your page so that the writing is upside down, but faceup, (b) turn your page over as if you're turning the page of a book, and (c) illustrate your journal entry. Display the finished projects on a bulletin board with the pictures facing out and attached only at the top. When students see a picture that they want to learn more about, all they need to do is lift the picture to read the student's journal entry. Title the display "Turning Points."

Name ______________________________ *Expressive writing*

Turning Points

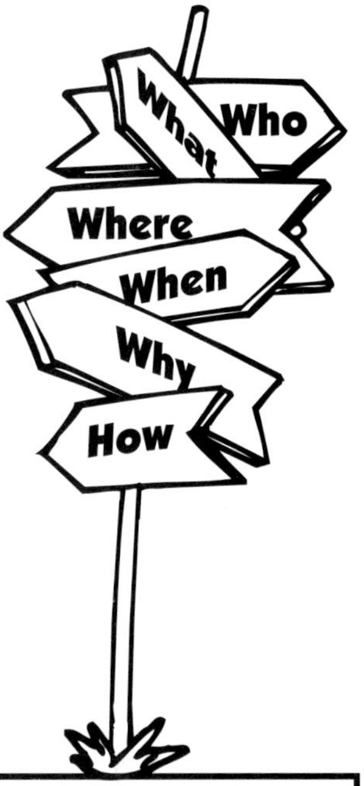

Who: ______________________________

What: ______________________________

Where: ______________________________

When: ______________________________

Why: ______________________________

How: ______________________________

Topic Sentence:

Your Feelings:
(Use sensory words and specific details.)

Conclusion:
(The significance of this event in your life.)

Time Capsule Memories

PROMPT

Pretend you have been asked to add information about yourself to a time capsule. Write a short autobiography for future generations to read.

Think It!

1. Describe to your students information you might add to a time capsule for people to find a hundred years from now. Include what is important to you, your likes and dislikes, and your hopes for the future. Then show students a photo of yourself that you would add to the time capsule.

2. Point out to students the differences between a biography (written about someone, by another person) and an autobiography (written about a person, by that person). Tell students that a person writes an autobiography to explain her feelings and beliefs and to record her life story.

3. Explain to students that expressive writing uses sensory details and emotions to share experiences and insights regarding people, ideas, places, and things. Then read aloud the prompt above, display it on a transparency, or write it on the board.

4. Give each student a copy of page 43. Have the student glue a picture of herself or draw a self-portrait in the picture frame. Then direct each student to record information about herself on the lines provided.

Write It!

1. Instruct each student to use the information she listed on page 43 to help her write an autobiography on another sheet of paper.

2. Encourage students to swap papers for peer response. After all changes have been made, direct the student to glue her picture frame from page 43 in the top right-hand corner of a sheet of parchment-colored paper (available at most office supply stores). Then have the student write the final version of her autobiography in the remaining space.

3. In advance, collect a class set of containers with lids (potato chip cans, tennis ball tubes, etc.). Then have each student cut out pictures and articles from discarded magazines or newspapers that represent the current year or have significance to her. Direct the student to glue the pictures on the parchment around her autobiography to form a collage; then have her roll the parchment paper into a scroll and tie it with a length of ribbon. Have each student place her scroll in a container and then decorate it to resemble a time capsule. Encourage students to take the time capsules home to keep for future opening.

Name _____

Time Capsule Memories

What are your hopes for the future?

_____
_____
_____
_____

Personal Word Bank
(Words that describe you and your feelings.)

Name: _____
Age: _____

What is important to you?

_____
_____
_____
_____

What do you like/dislike?

_____
_____
_____
_____

Name_____   *Expressive writing*

Student Response Sheet

To the Student: Use this response sheet during the proofreading or editing stage of your writing to help determine whether your writing uses specific and accurate sensory detail and emotions to share your experiences and insights. Give this response sheet and your writing to members of your peer response group. Read your writing aloud to your group. Have group members answer the questions in the spaces provided and then share their answers verbally. After considering group members' responses, make any changes you feel are necessary before writing the final version.

Title of Writing Selection:_____

Questions:

1. Which sensory images stick in your mind? _____
   _____

2. What thoughts and emotions do you think I was trying to express? _____
   _____

3. How did what I wrote make you feel? _____
   _____

4. What do you think was my main point? _____
   _____

5. Are there any parts that you did not understand? _____
   _____

6. Was there anything missing that you wanted to know? _____
   _____

7. What did you like best? _____
   _____

Think About It!

I think I did a _____ job of expressing my thoughts and feelings in this writing selection because…

_____

_____

_____

Expressive-Writing Response Sheet

Student's Name: _____ **Date:** _____

Title of Writing: _____

Teacher Response Items

1. The sensory images that stick in my mind are _____
   _____
   _____

2. The thoughts and emotions I think you were trying to express are _____
   _____
   _____

3. What you wrote made me feel _____
   _____
   _____

4. I think your main point was _____
   _____
   _____

5. I would like to know more about _____
   _____
   _____

6. The part I liked best was _____
   _____
   _____

Comments: _____
_____
_____
_____

Extra Prompts

1. Almost everyone has a secret place in his or her home, yard, or neighborhood. Think about what makes your secret place special. Using specific and accurate detail, write a letter to a friend describing your secret place and expressing your feelings about that place.

2. Not everyone likes the same kind of pet. Think about your favorite kind of pet. Write an essay expressing your feelings about what makes your favorite pet the best!

3. Do you like to wear brand-name clothes? Or do you have a style all your own? Write a journal entry describing the kind of clothes you like to wear and expressing your thoughts and feelings about wearing brand-name clothes.

4. Think back to a concert, play, or performance you have attended. Write a diary entry that expresses your feelings about what you saw and heard, including lots of specific and accurate detail.

5. Picture the best trip away from home you've ever taken. Write a travelog describing where you went and who went with you. Include detail about things you saw, heard, touched, smelled, and tasted along the way.

6. Imagine that it is 100 years in the future. Things in your neighborhood have really changed. Write a memoir describing the changes and expressing your thoughts and feelings about the changes.

7. Think about your favorite character from a book. Write a poem about that character with the title "Ode to [character's name]." Paint a clear picture of the character by including specific and accurate detail about what the character looks like, acts like, says, and does.

8. Recall a time when your favorite sports team won a big game. Write a journal entry describing the game and expressing how you felt when your team won.

Extra Prompts

9. Recall a time when a sister, brother, parent, grandparent, or other relative did or said something that really got on your nerves. Write a letter to the relative expressing your thoughts and feelings about what the person said or did.

10. It's time to change the rules! Choose a school rule that you would like to change. Write a short personal essay expressing your thoughts and feelings about why the rule should be changed.

11. Choose a cartoon from a newspaper. Decide whether or not you think it is funny. Write a letter to the editor expressing your thoughts and feelings about why the cartoon should or should not be removed from the paper.

12. Think back to when you first met your best friend. Write a journal entry expressing what you thought and felt about your future friend after your first meeting.

13. Moving to a new place can be exciting, uncertain, or scary. Write a personal essay expressing your thoughts and feelings about a time when you moved to a new home, community, or school.

14. Some people like to play games, some like to read, and some like to explore nature. What is your favorite thing to do? Write a diary entry about a day you spent doing your favorite thing.

15. Think about the most wonderful treat you ever tasted. Write a poem describing what the treat looked like, smelled like, tasted like, and felt like as you gobbled it up.

16. Imagine that you are 90 years old. Think back on all the things that you have experienced over your lifetime. Write a short memoir expressing your thoughts and feelings about the best day of your life.

Editing Symbols

Writers use special marks called *editing symbols* to help them edit and revise their work. Editing symbols are used to show what changes a writer wants to make in his or her writing.

Symbol	Meaning	Example
◯	Correct spelling.	animl
ℒ	Delete or remove.	dogg
◡	Close the gap.	f i sh
∧	Add a letter or word.	lives in tree
#	Make a space.	flies south
∿	Reverse the order of a letter, a word, or words.	plants eats
⋏	Insert a comma.	the crab an arthropod
⊙	Insert a period.	Cats purr
⋎	Insert an apostrophe.	a deers antlers
⋎⋎	Insert quotation marks.	She said, Look at the pig.
≡	Make the letter a capital.	birds eat seeds.
/	Make the letter lowercase.	a Snowshoe hare
¶	Start a new paragraph.	¶Some dogs have tails.